SELF-KNOWLEDGE

THE GOLDEN THREAD OF PEACE AND WISDOM

The Promise of Yoga	49
Wisdom at the Heart of Experience	54
Meditation Sessions	62 & 88
From Conflict to Harmony	65
Yoga in the Light of Modern Science	76
Recognizing the Thread	89

In this special Convention issue is reproduced the complete programme of lectures and meditation practices which were given at our Annual One-Day Lecture Course in October 1999 under the title of *Yoga — The Golden Thread of Peace and Wisdom*. The theme is developed progressively and consecutive reading of the articles is recommended. We hope that both those who attended the Convention and those who did not will enjoy the opportunity to read the text of the talks.

The Promise of Yoga
Introduction to the Annual One-Day Course

WE ALL like promises, especially if they lead to good things. The most pleasing promise speaks of benefits which will flow towards us, without our having to do anything about it. The other type of promise is that we will get benefits *if — if* we fulfil certain conditions.

The spiritual Yoga puts before us both kinds of promise. The first promise is like when we are told some great heart-warming fact by a friend, or by an expert who sees more than we do. It is the sort of promise where we say: 'No! It can't be true', and our friend says:

'I assure you — it *is* true'. In Yoga this promise is made to those who have begun to question, to wonder, to think twice about where they are heading, to ask: 'What am I? Is there a meaning? Is there a goal? Will I ever be happy?'

The Yoga promise in answer to these searching questions is: 'You are more than you appear to be. There is far more to life than you know. You have a spiritual Self, your innermost essence, which is already divine. Being divine, your true Self is already free, peaceful and perfect. It is one with all. You don't have to add anything to yourself. You have only to know yourself. You have only to acquire self-knowledge.'

If we say: 'No, it's just not true', the spiritual teachers, not just of Yoga but of all the great traditions, say: 'Assuredly — it *is* true'. But a kind of inner psychological mist is hiding this truth, just as the sun is sometimes blotted out by mist. The sun is not really blotted out. It only seems to be the case to those who are in the mist. This mist has many names: wrong thinking, wrong identification, distraction, attachment, habit, lack of enquiry, spiritual ignorance.

And this leads back to the second promise of Yoga, the type of promise which tells us we will get benefits *if* we fulfil certain conditions. This promise says that if we take up the methods of the spiritual Yoga — and take them up properly — the mist which hides the truth about our real nature will be dissipated. If we take steps to transform our mind and develop the inner peace and harmony, we will gradually uncover a fountain of peace and power springing from within ourselves. And if we take the trouble to enquire, to investigate more deeply into our own true nature, getting light and insight from the Yoga classics, we will find our true Self is raised above all change and suffering. It is free and universal, one with the golden thread of spiritual consciousness, cosmic consciousness, which is the hidden support of everything. We will not only get back in touch with the forgotten glory of our spiritual nature, but it will become the most immediate aspect of our experience.

The first promise — of our divine nature — is not unique to Yoga. If we look closely at all the authentic scriptures, listen carefully to the sincere voice of all the great sages and philosophers, we will not fail to hear the echo of the old affirmation: 'Grieve not, you are divine. Everyone is divine in his innermost nature. You are the crown of creation and you are planted in this universe to realize your essential divinity'. This universality of the spiritual teachings is one of the golden threads presented to us by the yogis.

But now we turn again to the second promise — the *if* promise of Yoga. The spiritual teachers have told us what we are in our true nature. The challenge is to become — that is, to unveil, to realize — what we really are, and this becoming or unveiling means work, chiefly inner work. It means transforming our own mind and learning how to manage our own inner life. And this is self-management of a very special nature.

There are courses in business management and these are very popular. As one mature student commented: 'This course in management studies enabled me to re-invent my career. I enjoyed watching my work take a quantum leap. The course changed me quite profoundly.' This shows a transformation, not just a career gain. The course uncovered, as all education uncovers, great hidden potentialities.

But there is another area of management which many of us overlook completely, and yet is the key to lasting happiness. This is the mastery of our own mind and emotions. This is not just a matter of control and good management. It is a conversion of the whole mental life into peace and wisdom. This course of management will give us something that no one can ever take away from us, and is not dependent on the approval or support of anyone else.

The promise of Yoga is to give us definite methods which, when used regularly and with a sincere desire for wisdom, will enable us to manage our lives, through managing our minds. If we follow up this Yoga, we will learn that yogic mind-management goes a very long way indeed and has wide and deep implications.

At first we will learn how Yoga can help us bring about those very desirable changes that we all want in our inner life: how not to be tortured by our own emotions; how not to feel limited or crushed by outer circumstances; how not to be afraid of others; how to feel unconditionally happy. These are all spiritual qualities which we can introduce into our minds. But these changes, which mean bringing harmony and order to our inner life, are a prelude to much higher and more worthwhile changes. Those changes are to do with spiritual enlightenment — the goal of Yoga.

We are now in a position to ask the question: 'Who is qualified to pursue the spiritual Yoga?' Does it depend on age, or health?

Does it depend on education or position? Do we have to be unusual or special? Do we need to know all about Indian culture? Do we need to change our religion or to join a new religion?

The answer to all these questions is 'No'. The two promises of Yoga make it clear that, essentially, everyone is qualified. Just as every single wave in the sea is qualified to 'become' the sea, so all human beings are qualified to re-discover the infinite reservoir of peace, light and happiness, which is the true nature of the deepest aspect of our being even now. Therefore everyone is qualified to take up the spiritual Yoga, provided they are interested in doing so.

In the *Bhagavad Gita* — the great classic of the spiritual Yoga — you will find a verse which says: 'Even a little of this Yoga brings immense benefits. Here no effort is ever wasted, and it can do no harm at all.' Yoga is not a new religion, but it is a practical path to spiritual wisdom, a wisdom which is at the root of all the great religions.

Perhaps a more important question is: 'Why bother at all?' Isn't it better to leave well alone, and get on with life? Shouldn't we concentrate on strengthening our material base — our security, on expanding our friendships, and perhaps widening our horizons through culture, study, travel, and so on. Why not sit back and enjoy the ever-growing range of amenities which are available to us? Why get involved with a spiritual culture which promises no outer advancement at all and, instead, holds out the possibility of an inner transformation which we know will require effort and dedication?

The answer is given in a verse from the Upanishads: 'When a man can roll up the sky like a piece of leather, only then will his sufferings be obliterated — only then will he be truly happy — without knowing the spiritual Truth.' The ancient sages recognized that human beings are not small-minded when it comes to what they really want. They knew that, deep down, behind all our small limited desires, there is one underlying and persistent desire which will have to be met some day or other. This is the desire for God-realization, complete freedom and enlightenment, which brings the certainty: 'At last, I know what had to be known. I have achieved what had to be achieved. I have found perfect peace.'

Finally we will ask: 'Does accepting the promise of Yoga — or the two promises: the affirmation of our own divinity and the claim that there are certain methods which will help us to realize it — does this mean that we let go of reason and surrender ourselves to some unproved dogma?' Worse still, are we expected to accept without question the unscientific statements put forward by teachers who flourished before humanity reached maturity?

The clear answer of Yoga is 'No'. We shall find echoes of yogic wisdom not only in religious writings, but in the insights of some of the greatest scientists and even in the most modern discoveries of science, which apprehends, in its own way, one fundamental principle underlying the whole universe. This is the golden thread peeping through at the sub-atomic and also the interplanetary levels.

But whether or not science endorses the spiritual doctrine of universal unity, we will only benefit from this insight when it becomes part of our own spiritual vision. Returning to Yoga, we are only able to realize the unity directly by diving deep into our own hearts. So we need to learn how to make a practical clearing in the inner world of our mind — a clearing of the mist — and this is one of the primary aims of the practice of meditation. As we said earlier, Yoga is fundamentally a process of becoming what we really are. A better word for 'becoming' would be recognizing, realizing. The golden thread does not need to be created. It is the hidden support and essence of all our experience. The thread can be recognized once the right inner conditions have been developed.

In conclusion, Yoga promises that the inner nature of each and everyone is divine, but this first promise is of little use without the second promise: that there is a method of realizing in experience this divinity. A modern teacher has said that it is like standing by a cow, and saying: 'Milk, milk, milk'. Yes, there is milk, but something has to be done in order to get it out, to release it.

The first promise is implicit in the name given to this Yoga: *Adhyatma Yoga*, the Yoga of Self-Knowledge, the Yoga aimed at revealing the immortal. The word *'adhyatma'* was once explained by Shri Shankara as 'that which first shows itself as the innermost Self in the body, and turns out in the end to be identical with the Supreme Reality, Brahman'. The second promise shows the way we can approach this Truth and make it our own experience and be free forever.

B.D.

Wisdom at the Heart of Experience
First talk of the Annual One-Day Course

THIS TALK is to offer you some of the ideas Yoga puts forward about wisdom. The key idea is that the highest wisdom is present in everyone. But it needs to be released through a practical path of inner training.

What is wisdom? It is a great word with many shades of meaning. In an ordinary sense, it means knowing how to deal with situations, usually based on long experience. It is wider and deeper than knowledge.

If the lights fuse in this hall, or the sound system breaks down, someone here with knowledge could probably put it right. But suppose the hotel had double-booked, and there were crowds pushing to take over this room for *their* meeting. How do you deal with such a situation? I think wisdom rather than knowledge would be able to handle it. Staying calm, knowing how to deal with people, maintaining good humour, above all, having the clarity of vision to quickly assess the situation and come up with a solution: all this needs a certain kind of wisdom.

Not surprisingly, wisdom is usually linked with experience or maturity. There is a sense that the wise person has 'been through it'. Wisdom is often associated with advanced years. Old people have lived through it; they know how it is. The problem here, as Shakespeare recognized, is that we need to get wisdom *before* we grow old. You remember in *King Lear*, the king had a fool, a court jester, who was licensed to say outrageous things to amuse the king. The king had a terrible shock, which unbalanced his mind. And the fool looked at the old man with pity and said: 'O Uncle, you've grown old before your time. You should not have grown old before you grew wise.' So seniority, old age, is not an automatic passport to wisdom.

Nowadays many people seek the help of counsellors. The value of a counsellor is that (we hope) they have some wisdom, and also they are not involved in our situation. They are detached. They can view our problems without getting emotional about them. In this way they may see a solution, a way forward, which we don't see. This is because our own emotions are a kind of inner fog which we can't see through. From this we learn that wisdom may have something to do with being able to stand back from ourselves, to disentangle ourselves from self-centred emotions, and to see what's going on in a more detached way.

People who are always giving advice are not necessarily wise. We've all met people who don't chat; they preach. Every phrase is a directive telling us what we should do, or should have done. Such people make us feel a bit uncomfortable. The English poet Coleridge occasionally gave sermons, and he once said to his friend, Charles Lamb: 'Charles, have you ever heard me preach?' 'Samuel — when do you do anything else?', was the reply. So in our quest for wisdom, we certainly don't want to become like that.

Then what is the wisdom we need, the wisdom at the very heart of experience, concealed in our own consciousness like butter concealed in milk? More important, what is the process by which we bring into manifestation this great force within us? The yogis say true wisdom is an emanation of our deeper spiritual nature, the nature which most of us are hardly aware we possess. Wisdom, at its source, is spiritual. It relates to our inmost spirit. And it is universal, meaning that there is no-one without this seed of wisdom in them. It's just a case of knowing how to feed and develop it.

Let me offer an illustration, based on a true report. Gold is not present everywhere. I read of an old gold seeker who worked in the rocky mountains in Canada. He loosened the rocks, usually with an explosive, then separated them into two piles. One pile he called gold. You couldn't see the gold, but he knew that these rocks were worth probing. The other pile he called *leaverite*. The interviewer said: 'Yes, I've heard of leaverite. Isn't it used in the building industry?' This man answered: 'That may be. But to me leaverite stands for one thing: It's short for *leave her right there — she ain't worth bothering with!*'

Now this may be true of rocks. Some have a natural endowment of mineral wealth, while others are quite worthless. But is not at all true of human beings. By virtue of what we are, by virtue of our consciousness — our very *experience* — there is something at the heart of us which is far greater than gold. This something is worth investigating. When probed and penetrated, it is called peace, conscious immortality, inspiration, higher knowledge, wisdom 'as firm as a mountain peak'. In other words, none of us is made of 'leaverite'. In fact, the sage Shri Dada of Aligarh used to say: 'The spiritual light is in all beings, and I am merely trying to turn their attention to this fact'. Attention means: *where* we look, and *how* we look.

Spiritual wisdom involves an earnest attempt to *look deeper*. Our founder, Hari Prasad Shastri, once said:

Wisdom is to see deeper than with the eye, and with sympathy.
Wisdom is to be aware of the golden thread which unites us all.

Such wisdom is not on the surface. Somehow, it is a seeing beyond the surface and finding there a hidden peace, a hidden harmony. The mystic Jalalu'ddin Rumi has said: 'The earth's face looks dull and sour, but inside every atom there is joy and hidden laughter'. We can fix our gaze on the surface, which is always changing and which very often presents us with a sour face. Or we can learn to see beyond this realm of change, to the spiritual dimension of peace, harmony, unity, joy — of hidden laughter.

What is the surface? The surface is what we see with our everyday mind and senses, and the values which condition our minds at this level of experience. The surface is judging people because of their skin, clothing, age or wealth. It is judging on appearances, or even on rumours. The surface is headlines, the commerce-driven world of the media, the stream of information about things which don't really matter. The surface consists of all the distractions we resort to, in order to avoid being alone with ourselves. The surface is glamour, romance, excitement, running from one stimulus to another, never spending time to reflect on the meaning of it all.

We have to live partly on this surface and give it attention. But the yogic advice is: 'Make use of it, but don't be hypnotized by its values of pleasure, power, name and fame'. These do not yield true joy, because such joy is always mixed with anxieties, and is vulnerable to interruptions and changes which can spoil everything. The gold of wisdom is not to be found on the surface.

The beginning of real wisdom is to suspect that there must be something more than the surface, something deeper, more reliable, which will never let us down, even if the world comes to an end. If the true treasure is not to be found on the surface, yet is present in experience, then where and how is it to be found? It is to be found within ourselves, in the depth of our own being. The solution is therefore introvertive. It urges us to dive deeper in the only place where we can dive deeper: in ourselves.

There is a mystery about what we really are, a mystery to be solved through self-discovery. It is all a question of learning how to turn our attention to the spiritual light at the heart of our own experience. This brings us to the inner realm of the mind, and I would like to offer you a further definition of wisdom given by Hari Prasad Shastri. He once said:

> Wisdom is to clean the glasses of the mind.
> Wisdom is to have an understanding of the 'I'.

This brings us a little closer to the heart of experience. Here the image is of the mind as a pair of spectacles. As we all know, spectacles get dusty and greasy unless we remember to clean them. In a similar way, when our mind is always focused on externals, and never turns within, it easily becomes fatigued, restless, stressed and anxious. When we get into this state, it is very difficult to have a clear idea of the situation. At times like this, we forget our great inner potentialities, and persuade ourselves that we are weak, limited and at the mercy of circumstances.

Another point that the yogis make is that the use of the human mind, and its value, is not just to reveal to us the outer environment. The mental energy, expending itself through the senses, does reveal to us the wonders of the world of nature. But that same mental energy, if it is withdrawn from the outer sphere, can reveal to us what one teacher has called 'the magic properties and greater wonders of the inner realm'. Cleaning the glasses of the mind means learning to wipe off the dust and grease formed by constantly worrying about outer situations and other people, and through losing ourselves in dreams or plans based on personal pleasure or advantage. The inner glasses only become clear and clean when we learn to forget the world and our personalities for a while, dive deep within our own being, and come in contact with the deeper realm of peace and light.

This change can only take place gradually, but once begun and pursued seriously, it is progressive. In the Shanti Sadan publication, *The Power Behind the Mind*, the way of progress is indicated:

> The whole progress of the learner has been from extreme and instinctive mental activity (generally of an extrovertive nature), to an inner, conscious and directed stillness, which bears little resemblance to the early, restless preoccupations of the untrained mind. This progress from mental noise to silence, from repletion to emptiness, is the way in which the expectant mind prepares itself for the coming of the spiritual truth.

This process of inner quietening, and what it reveals, is illustrated in the old story about the boys in the classroom. In an Indian village school, the boys were singing out their lesson, when a parent burst in and angrily said to the teacher: 'I can't hear my son singing the lesson. No wonder he is dull. He's not singing and you don't seem to care at all.'

The teacher said: 'Sir, just be quiet, please, and calm yourself. Now listen.' He then directed the children one by one to stop singing until, in the end, the voice of just one child remained: that was the voice of the so-called dull boy. The teacher commented: 'You couldn't hear his voice because of the surrounding noise. And you are a disbelieving sort of man, so you thought he wasn't singing. But when I created silence all around, then you could see clearly the truth of the situation. Indeed, all is well with your son, and he is a very promising pupil!'

This illustration shows that when we learn to slow down the fretful mental activity, something very deep, beautiful and blissful will be revealed in our experience — not as something new, but as something which was there all the time. Quieten the inner noise of desire and imagination, and the eternal presence will be revealed within.

When we begin to train the mind, as in meditation, we will find there are new challenges. Everyone has to face these challenges. They really concern the state the mind has got itself into through its habits of extrovertive living. The fact is, the surface glitter has claimed our attention and interest for so long that it has actually moulded our way of thinking. One result of this conditioning is felt when we first try to meditate. We think: 'Well, meditation will make me peaceful'. Then most of us find, not peace or relief, but a kind of inner arena, vibrating with sounds, images, colours and movement, and which is busier than Trafalgar Square on New Year's Eve.

One of the old Hollywood film directors was called before a sponsor, who said: 'This time I want you to make a film about Hollywood itself. Only, I want you to tear off the false tinsel.' The director, who had insight, replied: 'You mean you would like me to expose the real tinsel underneath!' In a similar way, in meditation we try to shut out the false glitter of the outer world, and find, to our dismay, that it's all still there underneath: the worries, the half-formed plans, the pictures, the restlessness, the agitation. It just doesn't stop. If our minds are very active, which is a sign of great inner energy, the inner restlessness appears to be intensified.

In the great classic, the *Bhagavad Gita*, the pupil, whose name is Arjuna, complains to the teacher: 'You prescribe meditation. I have tried it. But this mind just can't be controlled. It's impossible. It's like trying to control the wind.' The teacher, Shri Krishna, comforts him and says, in effect: 'You are right. The mind is very difficult to deal with. But if you persevere in your regular practice, and if you go on trying to defy the hypnotism of outer objects and attractions, changes *will* slowly take place within you. Your meditation will improve. It will deepen and, in time, become a source of very great joy. Just have faith in the practice and in your own deeper spiritual nature. Nothing worthwhile is the work of a day.'

How, then, do we discover the wisdom at the heart of experience? The plan of Yoga is to learn how to dive deep into our nature, to discover the real, the true Self whose nature is Pure Consciousness and Bliss. It is based on the conviction that the roots of the human mind do not exhaust themselves in the shadowy region of the Unconscious, as expounded by Freud. On the contrary, the source of mental life is the innermost region of the Spirit. The Chinese sage Mencius has written: 'He who gets to the bottom of his mind comes to know his own nature. Knowing his own nature, he also knows God.' This is a well-known experience in the East, and the basis of oriental spiritual culture. Here is another expression of it by the poet Han Shan:

> My mind is like the autumn moon
> Shining clean and clear in the green pool.
> No, that is not a good comparison.
> Tell me, how shall I explain?

If this area of experience interests us, or seriously attracts us, we have — by virtue of that very attraction — a golden handle, or guiding hand to help us through this inner world.

In fact, the way forward is nothing foreign or unnatural to human experience. It is really a question of learning how to redirect our existing powers, and give them a spiritual direction. Even on a very ordinary level, we can select more carefully from the sources of cultural nourishment available, and choose things which will help our inner peace. Anyone whose will has been awakened and galvanized through meditation practice, can learn to throw off silly and anti-social ways of acting and thinking, and become thoughtful and co-operative.

Some of you may have read about a man who was given to road-rage, but who turned himself into a creative peacemaker. This man used to get very angry and take it personally if he was overtaken, or if the car in front was moving too slowly, nearly getting into fights. Yet he came to realize that his anger was ruining his own peace of mind, quite apart from the misery he was causing others. Through this insight, he resolved to change his ways. All that angry energy was turned in a new direction. He put all his attention, and his savings, into inventing a new product: an illuminated display which sent, from his rear window, polite and friendly messages to other motorists. There were three simple signals: Sorry — Thanks — Help. In this way, the great force of human emotional energy was diverted from its silly and potentially destructive outlet, to become a harmonizing force. Wise re-direction, based on constant reflection on the spiritual teachings, is a fundamental principle of Yoga.

What is the final aim of Yoga? Yoga is not just concerned with individual or social peace, nor with improving our own character, though it helps in all these areas. The purpose of Yoga is insight into the nature of our own consciousness. As we heard, 'Wisdom means to have an understanding of the I, the true Self'.

We heard before how the best advisers are those not involved in our affairs, and who are therefore detached from the emotive issues which are agitating our hearts. In a similar way, Yoga says that our inmost Consciousness, the ultimate knower of the personality — that which is aware of the thoughts and emotions from within — actually transcends the mental operations and is free, infinite and one in everyone. This is the Power behind the mind. It has been called the innermost witness of the dance of the thoughts and the emotions, yet who is never involved in the dance, and who never appears on the dance-floor! This is one of the peak insights of Eastern mysticism, and it is an extremely practical insight, with great implications for the way we lead our lives.

The Japanese poet Basho had an understanding of this truth. He once stood on a hot night in a Japanese town, with throngs of people, horses, smells of cooking and so on. Looking above the town, he saw the summer moon. There it was: large, full, glowing, very beautiful, and completely untouched by the scene below. He wrote:

>   Above the town
>   Filled with the odours of things
>   The summer moon.

In the same way, all the Yoga classics say that above the mind, with its qualities, good or bad, its restlessness and its thirst for something higher and better, there is the pure I, the true Self, the Atman, the *Adhyatma*. It is already free and pure, and its nature is infinite consciousness and bliss. This is why the serious student of Yoga can affirm at any time: 'In my true nature, I am fearless. I am free, pure, peaceful and illumined even now'— like that full moon. Even to recall, now and then, this great fact, helps to clean the glasses of the mind, helps us to see deeper than with the eye, and brings us into touch with the wisdom at the heart of experience.

A.H.C.

ANNUAL ONE-DAY COURSE MEDITATION SESSION

Meditation has become very popular in the West. At one time it was considered odd and cranky. Not any more. There are many kinds of meditation or rather many reasons why it is practised. The meditation offered today is ancient and traditional. It has been taught in the East for thousands of years and its sole purpose is to approach the Divine who dwells within, and through knowledge to experience God directly. Meditation in this tradition is not practised for any material gain; not for health or even relaxation but solely to know by direct experience that Truth which is within all and supports and transcends all.

The aim of the practice offered today is the highest. It is a spiritual practice with a universal aim. It is not selfish in any way — on the contrary it will benefit more beings than can be realized. Yet it is perfectly safe to try. The aspirant will not be swallowed up in an experience he is not ready for. It takes time for the mind to be purified and eventually transcended. Yet each stage has its own unlooked for rewards along the way: greater peace of mind, contentment, tolerance, forgiveness, patience, and an increased yearning to know the Truth.

No two minds are the same. No two minds work the same. No two minds will meditate exactly the same and the only way to learn how to meditate is by doing it — which sounds obvious but when our Teacher was asked by a despairing pupil, 'How can I learn how to meditate?' his reply was: 'Meditate, meditate, meditate'. We learn by doing it, over and over and over and over again. Something other, be it a book, friend or even the spiritual teacher, can only help so far. The experience is a personal one and will be different for each individual according to the impressions made upon the mind by past experiences.

Do not expect to be able to sit down and go into deep meditation straight away. Only an adept can do that. As with everything else in life, in order to meditate there has to be preparation. Here are some yogic forms of preparation for meditation.

Rhythm

Choose a time. First thing in the morning is said to be best, before external impressions flood into the mind. Keep to the time chosen come what may. It will be recognized in time as the most important part of the day. It is just as easy to create a good habit as a bad one.

Posture

There is nothing mystical in this tradition about *the way* to sit in meditation. The aim is to find a position which is comfortable and can be held if necessary for long periods. When young and the body flexible, persevere with the cross-legged posture on the floor. It becomes the best in the end, where the body is balanced and can be forgotten. That is the aim — to forget the body and have no distractions from cramp, pins-and-needles or a stiff neck etc. When with age the body protests at getting down on the floor, then sitting on a straight-backed chair works just as well, with spine erect and both feet on the floor. Even on a chair a balance can be discovered and maintained.

Relaxation

Nothing worth while is ever attained in a state of tension. As you sit, drop the shoulders and feel all knotted tension drain away, leaving a calm and tranquil state. Do not slump though. The spine should always be erect but the body relaxed. Think of the shoulders as being like a coathanger from which the body hangs loosely like a jacket.

Attitude of Mind

It is very important when approaching the meditation period that the mind should be in the right frame. This time should be the holiest part of the day, when the mind consciously comes into the presence of God Himself within the heart. In truth we are always in the presence of God but mostly unaware of it. Here we wish to experience that presence and draw near.

Dr Shastri said 'We *must* meditate. That is to say, we must tutor our mind, and we must absorb our mind in something which is elevating; something which lifts the mind above the realm of the senses and brings it into touch with God within — that is the meaning of meditation and it is an essential part of our life'.

Aids

In order to help the right frame of mind it is good at first to prepare a place each day especially for the practice, with perhaps a statue or a picture of a saint or spiritual teacher or an incarnation of God like Jesus, Rama, Krishna. A lighted candle is a good thing to have on our little temple.

Another aid is to read a paragraph from a holy book with deep attention, like *The Imitation of Christ* or a few verses from a scripture like the *Bhagavad Gita* or the *Fourth Gospel*. All these were recommended by our Teacher.

The Practices

Begin then with an attitude of reverence and a salutation to that Power which upholds the universe and is the substratum of our own mind. Say a short prayer in your own words for guidance and light.

Next is the Breathing Practice which is a yogic exercise to still and quieten the extraneous thoughts. Take twenty-one deep breaths, imagining the breath being drawn up from the navel to the spot between the eyebrows. Relax consciously, without slumping, as the breath is expelled each time with no visualization.

The Lighted Candle is the second practice and it is to aid concentration. Look at a lighted candle, also in relaxation, for a few seconds. Do not strain. Then transfer that image to what is called the Heart Centre, the centre of the body where the ribs meet and gently concentrate on the form for five minutes.

Next is the Meditation Practice. Here is the text:-

OM. I AM THE INNER LIGHT WHICH PROMPTS THE MIND. I AM THE SUN WHICH LIGHTS THE WHOLE UNIVERSE. OM

Repeat the whole text interiorly several times extracting as much meaning from it as you can. Understand that the sun in the text is not the physical sun but the universal light of Consciousness. Then rest in the inner light without thinking of any words. The text is in two parts: personal then universal.

The thought of our daily meditation should eventually spill out into daily life until there is a constant remembrance of the Divine within.

It is important to end by radiating thoughts of goodwill to all beings, particularly to those who we think do not like us and vice versa. This goodwill we radiate could be in the form of light discovered within the meditation period.

S.O.N.

From Conflict to Harmony
Second talk of the Annual One-Day Course

THE STORY GOES that five men were once put in a dark room and asked to find out what object was inside. They each searched and fumbled in the pitch darkness and reached their conclusions. One said, 'It is a tree-trunk'; another said, 'It is a fly-whisk with a flexible handle'; another said, 'It is a snake like a python'; the fourth said, 'You are all wrong, it is a hard wooden spear'; the fifth said that it was a large fan. Disagreements, conflicts and arguments ensued, with none willing to consider the possibility that another viewpoint might have some value.

When a candle was brought to the dark room, the truth was revealed in the form of an elephant. One had mistaken a leg for a tree-trunk, another had taken the tail for a fly-whisk, a third thought that the trunk was a snake, the fourth had got hold of a tusk and the last who thought that the object was a fan, had hold of the ear of the long-suffering and extremely patient elephant.

The five men were mistaken because each only had hold of some aspect of the object, and they leapt to conclusions long before they should have done. It needed more time, more patience and more research, but then the mind of man has always had this tendency to seize upon the part and take it for the whole.

This story is very ancient and has had wide circulation. It is to be found in the *Masnavi* of Jalalu'ddin Rumi, the great Islamic mystic whose works are source books for many Sufi schools.

According to scholars, it is found in the works of the Jain religion. The Jains are known to us as the monks who sweep the ground in front of them as they walk in order to avoid harming any living creature. It is a religion as old as Buddhism and has much in common with it. But whereas Buddhism died away in India, the Jains survived, probably because they were content to use the services of Hindu priests in many of the ceremonies of daily life.

The story is also referred to by Shri Shankara, the great traditional authority on Adhyatma Yoga, in his commentary on the *Chandogya Upanishad*. The ancient literature of India is vast, beginning with the *Vedic Hymns* and moving on through the *Upanishads* which give us the wonderful debates held by the sages in the forest, through the *Puranas* to the epics of the *Ramayana* and the *Mahabharata* in which the *Bhagavad Gita* is to be found. Naturally, in such a wealth of material there are many apparent inconsistencies and difficulties. Shri Shankara wrote commentaries on the principal parts of this literature and his interpretation has always held the highest place in the orthodox tradition as the true reconciliation of the different viewpoints.

It is worthy of note that these traditions and genuinely great people all felt this tale worth retelling. They belonged to different faiths but human nature, whatever colouring of religion or culture it may give itself, always has some similar tendencies which need to be checked, and one of them is taking the part for the whole, and jumping to conclusions. It was a great belief of Dr Shastri that there is an underlying unity in all religions, and one of the meanings of the story is that the different faiths and the quarrels between them are like those men in the dark. The great saints have been able to speak the Truth to people of any religion or none. In our youth, we are all given some smattering of religious education. This mainly consists in people telling us that the leg of an elephant is a tree-trunk. The sages and saints are those whose own inner search leads them to realize what the tree-trunk really is.

We sometimes saw on television, thousands of Iranians shouting religious slogans on the streets of Tehran, denouncing the 'Great Satan' America. To our secular cast of mind there is something horrifying in the spectacle. But one ought to remember that it is really just a political pantomime which has nothing to do with the true religion of the heart and of the soul. The true saints of every faith have understood the inner demands of the faith they adhere to and have succeeded in rising to the challenge of those demands. In so doing, they receive an inner illumination which reveals the true meaning, grandeur and universality of their religion. The saints go beyond ideas and words to the Reality, like the founders of the religions. And if we examine what the founders say, they themselves do not claim to be starting anything completely discontinuous from the past. 'I come not to destroy but to fulfil' is their watchword. The Prophet Mohammed, on whom be peace, claimed to be the seal of the prophets, the last in line and the conclusion of the series. Hence the reverence in Islam for the Virgin Mary and the Prophet Issa or Jesus. When he returned in triumph to Mecca after his stay in Medina, he visited the Kaaba and went into the temple which housed the 360 idols worshipped by the pagan Arabs. He smashed them all except for two statues, the statues of Jesus and of Mary. He believed that his teaching was in the line of prophecy which stemmed from Abraham.

Nowadays, because a global view comes naturally to us, at least in theory, we can't help feeling that the squabbles between religions are parochial, even if we cannot sort them out ourselves, even if we cannot yet see the elephant for what it is.

The speaker takes it for granted that all present are in search of enlightenment, not a new set of clothes or slogans or creeds or a new way of getting one up on everyone else. Do we think a change of religion would help us? The great scholar and poet John Henry

Newman in the last century was a leader of the High Church Party in the Church of England. After appalling inner struggles and debates, he converted to Roman Catholicism. It was a tremendous shock to people of his Party. As the years passed it became clear that he was neither really welcome in the Roman Church nor happy. They called him a *'mauvais coucheur'*, a bad bedfellow, and when he started and ran the Catholic University in Dublin, the local Bishop had to reprimand him for the freedom which he allowed his students to visit the theatre and participate in the culture of the day. But Newman, with his background in the land of the free, believed that open-minded search for truth would lead everyone, as it had led him, into the fold. So when reprimanded, he always just said 'I will think about it'. No doubt he did think about it, but that was all, and in the end he had to be pushed out from his post, because the Roman Church at that time believed in close surveillance and restriction. There was and indeed is an index of books which are not to be read. Nobody could be trusted to behave themselves if given any freedom. Newman, whose use of his own freedom had led him to the Roman Church, was never quite at home.

So what we need is not a new set of religious clothes, but a new inner enlightenment. Yoga is not interested in external conversion. It is the inner world of man which needs to be changed. We have to start by admitting that we are in the dark. Our conceptions are very limited and our viewpoint is narrow. When astronomers bring the immensity of this amazing universe to our attention, and unfold a picture of solar system upon solar system, galaxy upon galaxy, many people become frightened, because their concerns are dwarfed into insignificance. But perhaps we can alter our concerns so that they are not dwarfed, but rather enhanced and encouraged by this vision of vastness. But they would have to be cosmic in scope.

Like the people who had hold of the different parts of the elephant, we are all intent on our individual lives as separate beings and we identify ourselves with finite limited bodies and minds. Perhaps our love of family gives us a feeling of connection with the past and future, but it doesn't go very far. We forget the manifest fact that we are all part of an intricate web of life which stretches from the inorganic minerals to organic life, we are all children of the sun and the earth, we all breathe the same air and walk on the same ground. We are all members of one another. Our idea of family is absurdly bob-tailed. We are all related to one another if you look back twenty generations. Perhaps we do not so much forget it as discount it. It doesn't seem important and significant. But here we betray a lack of imagination. Here we have a truth which we do not appreciate enough.

It doesn't seem to matter very much for practical purposes that although there is distinction, there is no ultimate separation, that we all belong together to this universe. It is just like the science of mechanics. In fact, as is acknowledged on the first page of every textbook, everything exerts a force on everything else. You cannot move a stone without troubling a star. Before you can even begin the study, you have to isolate a system of forces. Then you can do astonishing things, it is true. The predictions of the movements of heavenly bodies are exact to many decimal places. The Almanacs and Calendars are very precise. But the fact is, all the predictions could easily be disrupted by the appearance of a very large body in the vicinity of the solar system. It looks as though the astronomers have the heavens taped, but it isn't necessarily so.

Another example is found in agriculture. It is taken for granted that one can spray herbicides and pesticides at some level and suffer no ill-effects. But a study reported recently that the rain in Switzerland, that cleanest of countries, had more parts per million of several pesticides than was permissible in drinking water. It is a sad day when you cannot drink the rain that falls from heaven. There is no separation in the natural world, and whatever one neglects will come back and haunt him one day. Isolation is impossible.

There is no need to multiply examples. The source of conflict among and within human beings is the tendency to isolate themselves mentally from others and oppose their private interests to those of other people. The great Swami Rama Tirtha was both a scientist and a mahatma and a short biography of him was written by Dr Shastri. He wrote that the purpose of science was to discover unity in variety, and to establish that oneness intellectually.

Newton established that the falling of an apple from a tree and orbiting of a moon round the earth are governed by the same law of gravitation. Aristotle thought that these two types of motion were essentially different. Science proceeds by discovering deeper unities. According to Swami Rama Tirtha, the aim of religion is similar:

> The very purport of religion is to show and preach a oneness or unity in the whole universe. But in this respect there is one difference between science and religion. Science proves physical oneness experimentally and intellectually, while religion makes you realize the spiritual oneness practically and by actual living. The observations of science depend on the sense-organs, because science deals with names and forms. On the other hand, religion, because it makes one directly realize the truth about Atman, utilizes the inner eye, which bestows light on the physical eyes.

So the purpose of religion, according to Yoga, far from enhancing our sense of difference from others, that I am I and you are you, is to deepen our appreciation of the neglected unity and oneness of things. We have to admit that we are part of the great web of life, as we are joined by myriad connections to all around us. Our dependence on the world for sustenance is symbolized by the umbilical cord through which all our nourishment came when we were in the womb. We receive from the world and we make our contribution in some form to the world. Would we not be happier if we could feel this oneness? Would the contribution not be given more willingly and freely if we felt this unity?

What is the yogic cure for this condition of separation, this isolation, this self-centredness which afflicts us? It is the word 'Self' which gives the clue. Everything hangs on what we believe ourselves to be. In the Sanskrit language, the word for 'Self', as is very well known, is 'Atman'. This word can refer to many different parts of the human being according to the context. It can mean the body, the mind, the spirit. So if we replace the word 'Self' by 'Atman', and talk about 'Atman centredness', that too could mean a variety of things. Atman can be identified, or made the same as, many things. The central teaching of Yoga is that it is consciousness which is most myself, so to speak, and it is identifying oneself, one's Atman, with anything less than consciousness which causes all the conflict, suffering and loneliness in our experience. Consciousness is one and the same everywhere, one without a second and to have a glimpse of the unity of all things is to have a glimpse of the nature of consciousness. Consciousness is also unbounded, and intrinsically blissful. The Yoga teaches that we know this when we give up misidentifying ourselves with what we are not.

We can see that if we identify ourselves with a particular body, we have the logical corollary that we are finite and mortal and distinct from all other bodies. We will be in competition with them for scarce resources, as the economists say. So I am not just this body. For further evidence, we can see that athletes attain great command over their bodies. Something in them, the soul, commands the body to push on past the limits which it asserts at every step. 'I can't, I can't, I can't', says the body as the twentieth mile of the marathon approaches. 'Oh, yes you can. Oh yes you can, and you will', says the soul. Likewise explorers and mountaineers take pleasure in the hardships they endure on their expeditions. The interests of the body can be over-ridden. This assertion of soul-power, of will-power, over the body is a great feature of the ancient religions of India. The Jains who were mentioned before, at least the monks among them, attain their inner strength and eminence by resisting the demands of the body, and inflicting what seem to be tortures on themselves. It is a way, perhaps misguided, of proving to oneself that one is not just a lump of flesh.

Dr Shastri did not advocate this kind of behaviour, and his great pupil Miss Waterhouse used to say that moderation was the highest austerity. But they did teach non-identification with the body and indeed the mind. The mind is subject to observation and is just as much an object as the body, although it is more lively and intelligent. All our thoughts, ideas, feelings and dreams are within the mind, and the cast of our mind determines to a very large extent the kind of experience of life which we enjoy or suffer. Just as the body needs to be looked after, so does the mind if it is to be kept in a good state, as it may have many tastes and tendencies detrimental to its wellbeing. Nutritionists say that farm animals are better fed than many human beings because more care and thought is given to the composition of what they eat than most people give to their own diet. What to say of the food for thought we give ourselves! We should feed our minds with that company which brings out the best in us.

The worst thing for the mind is to spend all its energy in the service of the body's interests and tastes, because that is to enslave the higher to the lower. The possibilities of the mind, in terms of range and understanding, outstrip the possibilities of the body manifold. It is the power of thought, of speech, of mind which distinguishes us most clearly from the animal world. There are qualities such as wisdom and insight which may attend the mind, and perhaps the most valuable of all, Self-Knowledge and Self-Understanding. We cannot understand that with which we are identified, so I am not the mind, nor am I the thoughts, feelings and sensations which arise within it. The motions of the mind can be watched like the motions of particles in a cloud-chamber. As we grow up we get a better understanding of their significance. We spot a motion of jealousy or anger in the mind. Why does it arise? We believe that somebody has taken something away from us, be it a material object, some status, some place in the affections of another. We see a feeling of love or affection. We have seen some quality or attribute in somebody else and we wish to associate ourselves with it. We also have stirrings of conscience, some intimation of a higher calling, some true desire to transcend our present limitations. We know we ought to move forward in a certain direction. We ought to look more deeply into something. When it has been stilled and calmed, when its point of view is wide and encompasses not just one's little self, but the welfare of all creatures, the mind can tell us effectively what we ought to do and how to behave, how to make our individual contribution to the whole. There is nothing like excitement and agitation for making bad decisions.

So the mind, in a good condition, helps us in our lives, just as the body helps us in our purposes. But it is still an instrument. It is not the essential self. I am not the mind. So what am I? This is the great philosophical and practical question of life. The Yoga can give the answer in words, that you are the witnessing-consciousness, the point of subjectivity, that everything depends on this consciousness and that it is unlimited, blissful and untainted by anything else. It is the same in everyone, it is the canvas on which the picture of the world is painted, it is that of which everything is made, like the bubbles which are made of water. It is the source of the experience of unity, it is the end of all conflict and the basis of all harmony. The realization of this truth is the *raison d'être* of the Yoga from time immemorial. When we take to the practice of Yoga with enthusiasm and determination, we find the grand significance beginning to unfold in spite of our manifest limitations and weaknesses.

These are not statements which can be heard in a pub, and indeed, until this century, the central truths of the Adhyatma Yoga would not have been available in the Western world at all, even in a library. The modern world is rich in many ways. We are all acquainted with several systems of religious and philosophical thought. So why should this Yoga be given special privileges? Isn't it just one more system among so many? The modern world is hesitant of commitment. With so many to choose from, it is hard to make a choice. So no choice is made and nothing is understood. This is like someone who says, 'One person says it's a tree-trunk, one person says it's a fan, another says it's a snake — so they are all talking nonsense'.

But a full commitment to any of the faiths will bring great rewards to anyone. The speaker remembers a conversation with a man who said that when he began going to Church, he found that he was able to sleep properly again. A full commitment combined with real inward search would bring realization, because if you seek, you will find. The great advantage of the Yoga is that it tells you the Truth of your own Self, without any prevarication, from the beginning and gives clear means of realization.

A.S-B.

THE ANNUAL ONE-DAY COURSE CONTINUES ON PAGE 76

A SHOWER OF BLOSSOMS

from Hari Prasad Shastri

Meet the world carefree;
Do thy best and trust the infinite force
Which shapes the Spring and the Autumn.
Today is not all;
It is a tiny bit of the Infinite.
Courage, courage, as the Greeks say.
And patience.

> The spiritual wisdom is different from the worldly wisdom.
> Inner silence, accompanied by self-effacement,
> gives the light of the spirit.

Why does the cosmic intelligent force
Shut up the beautiful blossoms in the earth?
I think, to remind us that Beauty and Truth abide in all objects.
Nothing is dead, ugly, or in complete darkness.
See God in all, and He will manifest Himself to you
In flowers, trees, rivers and the stars.

> Reflect on His Maya, and smile;
> Do not try to understand it by reason.
> Sing like the dove; 'Thou art One'.
> No grief should overpower thee,
> No joy should possess thee.
> Calmly say: 'OM, OM, OM'.

What worthwhile gain is there in this passing world
If not mastery over one's mind and devotion to God?
Struggle onwards and restrain the senses
From lingering on the outside objects.
   Knowest thou what the nightingale of the dawn
    whispered to me: 'What sort of man art thou indeed,
                   who art ignorant of Love?'

        There is a blossom in each bud,
     And a thousand buds and blossoms in a seed.
          So is the world in thy Self,
    The Transcendent, the infinite Consciousness.

He is everywhere — in all. He is your Atman.
Take the changing circumstances as dreams,
And laugh at their ridiculousness.
None, none is dependable that functions in time-space.
The Self alone is dependable.
Courage, patience, dispassion.

    Unless you can get beyond the mind-consciousness and
experience, you cannot know the Truth of Absoluteness of Self.
       Mind is inert. Who animates it?
   The substance behind the mind must be transcendent —
                Brahman.

Vacancy
   Wanted: Lovers of Truth.
   Qualifications: Self-surrender, calm contemplation, detachment.
   Salary: God vision.
   Apply in solitude to your own Self.

Yoga in the Light of Modern Science
Third talk of the Annual One-Day Course

IN SITTING DOWN to listen to a lecture on Yoga in the Light of Modern Science, you may very reasonably be asking yourself: 'Can something as old as Yoga have anything to tell us that we do not know already or that is not rendered out of date by the modern discoveries of Science?' One answer to this is that, contrary to what you might suppose, a number of important things that we imagine have only just been discovered in modern times were already well-known to the followers of Yoga many centuries ago.

Let me give you three specific examples. Most people will tell you, if asked, that we owe the discovery of the existence of the unconscious mind and the recognition of its major influence on our conscious thoughts to Dr Sigmund Freud in this century. But this is not so. The unconscious mind and its influence on our conscious mind was well-known to the yogis long before Freud discovered it, and it is described in detail in the classical writings of Yoga.

Another very recent development in the West is the scientific study of sleep, which has revealed that there are not just two distinct states, wakefulness and sleep (with dreams occurring as a minor incident during sleep), but three quite distinct states: waking, deep sleep and dreaming.

The modern pioneer in this field of scientific investigation was Professor Nathaniel Kleitman in Chicago, who died as recently as August 13th this year at the age of 104 and whose obituary appeared in *The Times* on September 30th. His research work has shown clearly that there are three states of consciousness, with a distinct pattern of electrical brain waves characteristic of each. These states correspond to what we call deep sleep, dreaming and waking. The electro-encephalograph and associated physiological recordings show that they are characterized respectively by the presence of slow waves in the brain during deep sleep, changing to a quite different pattern associated with rapid eye movements during dreaming (so-called REM or 'rapid eye movement' sleep), and the well-known pattern of desynchronised waves and the alpha rhythm during wakefulness. One can follow the pattern of these three states as they change from one to another repeatedly throughout the night. In terms of brain physiology, sleeping is now characterized as 'fore-brain sleep', and REM sleep as 'hind-brain sleep', as these two regions of the brain appear to take their rest at different times, rather than together. The hind-brain is known to be particularly concerned with the centres controlling the body musculature, while it seems likely that the forebrain is 'awake' for the conscious experience, whether of dreams or the waking world.

A number of new and unexpected findings have been revealed by these brain-wave recordings. Before Kleitman's study, for instance, there was a widespread idea in the West that the actual time of dreaming had no relation to the time experienced in the dream, and that even long dreams occupied episodes lasting only a few seconds, but Kleitman showed that this was not so. The duration of the dreaming state, as evidenced by the brain-wave patterns, lasts roughly the same length of time as the dream experience reported by the subject when they are awakened.

These three distinct states were known to the yogis since ancient times, and are clearly represented in the symbol OM. The *Upanishads*, which are among the most ancient books of the world, describe all three states in detail. In the Sanskrit symbol, the different states of consciousness are represented by the varying length of the three curves, with the waking the longest (the lowest curve of the three); the deep sleep state (the upper curve) being somewhat shorter than the waking state (lower curve); and the dreaming state represented by the shortest curve arising from the junction of the other two. The symbol also shows the unbounded circle and dot representing what Yoga calls the fourth state or *turiya*, known to the awakened practicants of Yoga.[1]

The third example of an even more fundamental scientific truth anticipated by the yogis is the idea that the whole world of matter

---

[1] The symbol OM appears on the front cover of each issue of *Self-Knowledge*, and a fuller, illustrated description of its depiction of the different states of consciousness appeared in the last issue *(Vol. 51 No 1. Winter 2000 p 4)*.

and mind is fundamentally made up of the energy of Nature — something only demonstrated scientifically in this century by the revolutionary investigations of Einstein. Einstein showed in his famous equation, $\mathbf{E=mc^2}$, that matter and energy were interconvertible, and that energy was the fundamental 'stuff' from which the whole cosmos was made. The Vedanta philosophy has been teaching the same principle since ancient times — holding that the objective and mental worlds are a product, not of matter, but of the energy or creative power of Nature (*Prakriti Shakti*).

Yoga is also like science in being experimental, and in regarding its authority as direct experience, *not* faith or belief. A great modern yogi, Swami Rama Tirtha, makes this very clear, when he says:

> Vedanta is an experimental science like chemistry. In chemistry you cannot make any progress unless you make corresponding experiments. Similarly, what can a man know of Vedanta who does not perform spiritual experiments alongside the intellectual training that he gets.
>
> [*In Woods of God-Realization, 8th edition, Vol.3, p 119*]

> Authority cannot establish truth. A simple mathematical truth gains no more weight if Christ, Mohammed, Buddha, Zoroaster, the Vedas, all testify to it. Truth is to be *known* directly, not to be *believed* in.
>
> [*Woods, Vol.2, p 211*]

The goal of Yoga is personal verification by experiment and knowledge of the truth.

'This is all very well and good', you may say. 'No doubt Yoga and science share many things in common, but of what interest or relevance is Yoga to us in the modern world?' Our reply must be that Yoga is, in fact, intensely relevant to the modern world and its problems, particularly at this juncture. Let me try and explain why this is so.

The late Professor Colin Cherry of the Imperial College of Science and Technology pointed out that the 19th century had been the Century of Energy, in which man had for the first time harnessed the power of coal and steam to build his industries and drive his railways and had discovered electricity, and the electric motor and dynamo, which were to bring him light, heat and power in abundance.

In contrast with this, said Cherry, the 20th century had been the Century of Information, when communication had been rendered possible world-wide by telegraph, radio, television and now (one may add) by the internet.

Perhaps we can hopefully anticipate the 21st century being the Age of Enlightenment, the century in which man learns to live wisely, through an understanding of his own nature, i.e. by acquiring deeper Self-knowledge.

What is really interesting about science at the present time is that this whole area — the understanding of the nature of consciousness and its states — is currently becoming the main focus of attention among many scientists. Some of us would feel like adding: 'And about time too!'

We will return to this new scientific interest in a moment, but first, a word about the early pioneers of this awakening. Only a few scientists in the earlier part of this century have taken any real interest in consciousness and its different states, and in particular mystical experience — (Arthur Eddington and Erwin Schrödinger being notable exceptions). But William James in the late 19th century was among the first of the competent scientists to address this subject seriously as an area worthy of research. He gave the Gifford Lectures in 1901 and 1902 in Edinburgh on *The Varieties of Religious Experience*. These were published as a book in 1903 which has become a classic. He mentions Yoga in these lectures, although only briefly, but he deals extensively with accounts of mystical experiences from a wide variety of sources. He was not, however, himself a practicant of any of the techniques of meditation which he describes, nor apparently did he have any mystical experiences of his own to report. But he studied carefully the accounts of those who had had them, as a physiologist and psychologist who had trained as a doctor and scientist in Harvard University.

His main conclusions are given towards the end of the book, where he asks the question whether we can regard the evidence of mystical experience as authoritative. In answer to this he makes three points:

> As a matter of psychological fact, mystical states of a well-pronounced and emphatic sort *are* usually authoritative over those who have them. They have been 'there' and know.[2]

This last remark is a reference to the famous saying of the Neo-Platonist philosopher and mystic, Plotinus, about his own philosophy: 'Only he who has been there will understand my teachings'.

But William James reasonably adds the reminder that

> mystics have no right to claim that we ought to accept the deliverance of their peculiar experiences, if we are ourselves outsiders and feel no private call thereto. The utmost they can ask of us in this life is to admit that they establish a presumption.[3]

But he accepts that mystical states cannot simply be dismissed. Their reality has to be accepted and taken into account. His actual words are:

> Yet, I repeat once more, the existence of mystical states absolutely overthrows the pretension of non-mystical states to be the sole and ultimate dictators of what we may believe.[4]

It is perhaps not surprising that after this open-minded but cautious appraisal, scientists largely steered clear of the area. But in the last twenty-five years there has been an ever-increasing interest in investigating the subject of consciousness and a gradual lowering of the hackles which had greeted any attempt to introduce it for so long.

Professor John Searle expresses this scientific resistance well, when he writes:

---

[2] William James *The Varieties of Religious Experience*. Longman, Green & Co: London, 1903. p 423.

[3] Idem p 424.

[4] Idem p 427.

As recently as a few years ago, if one raised the subject of consciousness in cognitive science discussions, it was generally regarded as a form of bad taste, and graduate students, who are always attuned to the social mores of their disciplines, would roll their eyes at the ceiling and assume expressions of mild disgust.

The change in the climate of scientific opinion has occurred partly because, since about 1975, a number of eminent and first-rate scientists have begun taking a real interest in the investigation of consciousness and the self.

Let me give three instances. In 1977 the Nobel prize-winning physiologist, Sir John Eccles, and the philosopher, Sir Karl Popper, combined forces to produce a book on *The Self and its Brain*.[5] In 1994 the 83-year-old physicist, Francis Crick, another Nobel prize-winner, published a book, *The Astonishing Hypothesis*, which he subtitled *The Scientific Search for the Soul*,[6] in which he enthusiastically urges scientists to start investigating the nature of consciousness now! In the same year Roger Penrose, Professor of Mathematics at Oxford, published a book entitled *Shadows of the Mind: A Search for the Missing Science of Consciousness*.[7] These three examples suffice to show that contemporary scientists of the first rank are at last becoming interested in consciousness and inner states of mind.

But, as usual, when one looks again more carefully, one finds that some far-seeing members of the scientific community were alive to the importance of this area much earlier. One such individual was the great authority on Evolution, Sir Julian Huxley, who summed up his conclusions towards the end of his life in an article on 'The Destiny of Man', which appeared in *The Sunday Times* on September 7th

---

[5] J C Eccles and Karl Popper *The Self and its Brain*. Springer-Verlag: Berlin, 1977.

[6] Francis Crick *The Astonishing Hypothesis: The Scientific Search for the Soul*. Simon & Schuster: London, 1994.

[7] Roger Penrose *Shadows of the Mind: A Search for the Missing Science of Consciousness*. Oxford University Press. 1994.

1958. He spoke of the future of human evolution. His theme was that man, uniquely among the biological kingdom, had the course of his future evolution in his own hands and that it was he himself who must consciously bring about the next stage of his own progress towards the goal of fulfilment. 'The idea of the Welfare State (he said) must be supplemented by that of the Fulfilment Society.'

> He [man] can influence the process [of his own further evolution] only by understanding it and how it works, and for this he must apply the methods of science to its perplexing phenomena.
>
> The fuller his knowledge of its detailed workings, the more control he will have over them; the more comprehensive his understanding of the general process, the better he will be able to steer it in a desirable direction...
>
> Lastly there is religion. The world seems due for sweeping religious changes, with old religious systems fading away and new ones being evolved. So far as I can see, the only chance of securing a religion which will unite humanity instead of dividing it is to build it round the concept of evolutionary fulfilment, with belief in human possibilities as its central core and scientific method as its chief weapon. Yet mystery remains; we cannot prophesy the strange new possibilities that the psycho-social process will certainly bring forth.

Of fulfilment he says:

> It implies the attempt to understand more about man's inner life. How can man resolve psychological conflict, how attain peace and spiritual harmony? What is the value of 'mystical' experiences of self-transcendence, and can the techniques of attaining them, like Yoga, be readily communicated and learnt? We must follow up all clues to the existence of untapped possibilities...They may prove to be as important and extraordinary as the once unsuspected electrical possibilities of matter.

Here again we have one of the leading figures of his time in the biological field, recognizing the great interest and potential importance of the Yoga teachings and techniques, long before the subject of consciousness and the Self had become fashionable in scientific circles.

I hope that what you have already heard in the other lectures today has convinced you of the answer to one of Huxley's questions: the one as to whether the techniques of Yoga can be learnt or not. We who are fortunate enough to be pupils of Dr Shastri have no doubt that the answer is 'Yes!'. Huxley also shows himself to be one of the scientists who, even in the fifties, had become aware of the interest and importance of understanding the nature of consciousness. With regard to what Yoga has to say on the subject, I cannot do better than quote to you from Marjorie Waterhouse's book *Training the Mind through Yoga*:

> Consciousness — life — infuses every atom, but its existence could not be guessed without a medium of manifestation. It was so with the force of electricity, for instance. Men went on for thousands of years unconscious of the tremendous power which interpenetrated them, until its existence was revealed by science through an agent — matter. When we see consciousness in manifestation, we label it life, love, destruction, beauty, death, knowledge, and only know it as such and so limit it. Each of these qualities is a symbol of something greater, but as long as man thinks that they are the reality itself, his growth is retarded. Through worshipping the Lord in the symbol, you come to the reality behind the symbol, and this is the true mode of progression.[8]

The scientist is a worshipper of truth, and his approach through scientific enquiry and experiment is to find out the true nature of the object which he is examining.

Nowadays we have to remind ourselves that before about 1800 electricity was hardly recognized as of any great importance. Earlier than this it was only in a few exceptional circumstances that it manifested itself, most of all perhaps in the awe-inspiring lightning of the thunderstorm, which the common people regarded superstitiously as evidence of a supernatural visitation. This is certainly how Shakespeare depicts it, both in his verse...

---

[8] pp 127-128.

> Fear no more the lightning flash
> Nor the all-dreaded thunderstone.[9]

...or in King Lear's words in the thunderstorm on the heath at night, where he pictures it as a divine retribution visited upon evil-doers:

> Let the great Gods
> That keep this dreadful pudder o'er our heads
> Find out their enemies now. Tremble thou wretch
> That hast within thee undivulgéd crimes
> Unwhipped of justice.[10]

Apart from lightning and the mysterious northern lights (*aurora borealis*), only the strange properties of amber and the magnet with its ability to point north (discovered by the Chinese, and introduced into Europe in the 11th century) provided evidence of the existence of something out-of-the-ordinary and unexplained which we later came to call electricity.

But then after the pioneering scientific investigations of Michael Faraday and James Clerk Maxwell in the 19th century, it became clear that electricity was a fundamental phenomenon, all-pervading and deeply concerned with the chemistry and physics of all matter and indeed of the universe as a whole. Even so, it was not until 1880 that Hertz discovered the radio waves predicted by Clerk Maxwell and paved the way for advances which have now taught us that electro-magnetic energy is the fundamental material out of which the whole universe of time, space and causation is made.

The yogis predict that the same sort of thing will turn out to be true of consciousness when we have fully understood its fundamental nature. It will, they say, be discovered to be the essential nature of the real Self of man — each and every man — and of the universe.

We can also learn from science another valuable lesson. It is often felt that if, as the yogis say, this truth can only be verified by the individual in his own experience in the state of advanced

---

[9] *Cymbeline* 4.2.217-271.

[10] *King Lear* 3.2.49-53.

meditation, it is impossible to verify in the scientific sense and therefore must be regarded as something which can only be appreciated by the exceptional individual. If we think this, we would do well to remember the history of Einstein's Relativity.

Einstein himself discovered Relativity by thinking about the picture of time, space and what we mean by the *simultaneity* of events, for ten years before he produced his Special Theory of Relativity, and for another ten before he produced his more comprehensive General Theory in 1915. He himself was not a practical experimentalist, but knew all the scientific data very well. After arriving at his theory, he never showed any great interest in verifying it in any other way. To him the truth was plain and obvious.

Because the predictions of Relativity gave more or less the same quantitative conclusions as Newton's laws of motion in more than 99% of the ordinary observations — especially for objects moving at the sort of speed that we were able to measure at that time — many people did not believe his theory. It was only when other thinkers like Eddington were able to find special circumstances in which the predictions of Relativity and Newtonian physics gave measurably different results that the scientific attempt to find out which was the correct theory became possible and Einstein's theory was experimentally verified.

There were two main ways in which this was initially done. One was by studying a phenomenon which could not be explained by Newton's laws: the perihelion of Mercury — the way that the point at which the planet Mercury came nearest to the sun, in making its orbit round the sun, rotated slowly at a rate of 43 minutes of arc a year — not a very obvious event! It was found that Relativity predicted this rotation exactly, while Newtonian physics did not.

Then it was realized that, if, during an eclipse of the sun, one could observe the light from a distant star behind the sun just before it disappeared or appeared behind the sun, it would be possible to measure from the apparent position of the star whether the rays were being deflected by the gravitational pull of the sun in the way that Einstein predicted. A very much smaller deflection was predicted by Newton's theory. In 1919 scientists went out to Guinea in West

Africa and Brazil — places where they could see the eclipse: their observations were found to accurately mirror Einstein's prediction, showing clearly that Einstein was right and Newton wrong. This was confirmed in a second eclipse in 1922.

Here you have a very clear example of how it was only in exceptional and very special and unusual circumstances (a solar eclipse with a convenient distant star to locate accurately) that the truth of Relativity could be verified. But the fact is that Relativity is true at all times and places and is now recognized as an important factor in understanding the laws underlying the whole universe. Only when experimentally verified in these very special circumstances was it accepted by the whole scientific community.

Yoga maintains that consciousness is a fundamental element in the constitution of the whole universe, even though to the ordinary eye it is seen only in living things and in our own inner experience in the waking and dreaming states. But it is only in the exceptional circumstances of enlightenment that the enlightened yogi can clearly verify its more fundamental role.

But I must not leave you with the idea that Yoga and science, in spite of the many characteristics which they share, are identical in their methods of approach to the truth. It is true that both Yoga and science seek the one reality behind many phenomena. But science seeks it in the outer sphere, while Yoga seeks it within the personality. It is, in fact, only there that consciousness can be adequately studied.

Furthermore, the two disciplines do not share the same methods, as a great modern yogi, Swami Rama Tirtha, makes clear:

> Science proves physical oneness experimentally and intellectually [he says], while religion makes you realize the spiritual oneness practically by actual living. Neither science nor Yoga is content to remain reliant on hearsay evidence, they want direct verification.
>
> But here too, there is a slight difference. The observations of science depend upon the sense organs because science deals with (the outer objects characterized by) their names and forms. On the other hand Yoga aims at the direct realization of the truth, making use of the inner eye which bestows light on the physical eyes.
>
> [*Woods, Vol.5, p.11*]

He puts the matter very simply when he says that

The sceptical agnostic who decides that consciousness is something which he will investigate for himself scientifically (by the normal methods of science) is like someone who says: 'There is light in this match of mine. We must discover where it is.' So he cuts the match into little pieces and cannot find the light. He pulverises the match, but he still cannot find where the light is.

In the same way he goes on to say that there is life in the body, and he must find out where it is. But if he takes the body to pieces, he still will not find where the life is.

When it comes to consciousness, and the teachings of the Yoga, if there is a reality called consciousness, and I am that, let me find it, but he finds that it is unknowable by his mind.

[*Woods, Vol.3, p.50*]

But Swami Rama Tirtha says:

As long as we try and use the local consciousness of the individual ego to know the infinite, we can never know it. It is only when we have developed that cosmic consciousness that we can know it.

There is an Upanishadic verse on this topic with which I will end:

> Not by long study of the scriptures,
> Not by agile feats of intellect,
> Not by obedient listening to the wise
> Cometh the spirit.
>
> To him alone the spirit shall be given
> Who thirsteth for it,
> Who wooeth it untiringly,
> To such a seeking soul
> In very sooth the spirit cometh.

S.D.S.

ANNUAL ONE-DAY COURSE 2nd MEDITATION SESSION

The Meditation Practices described earlier on pages 62-65 were repeated at this point and the audience were given a 'Meditation Practices' sheet to take home. This is reproduced on page 95 of this edition of Self-Knowledge.

A further explanation of the meditation text is printed below.

OM. I AM THE INNER LIGHT WHICH PROMPTS THE MIND. I AM THE SUN WHICH LIGHTS THE WHOLE UNIVERSE. OM

There is something that gives us a sense of identity through all our different bodily states from infancy to old age, through all our different thoughts, feelings and experiences and in all the states of experience — our waking state, our dream state and our dreamless sleep state when the mind is not operating. It is constant and unfluctuating and witnesses the flux of all our states. The sages say that the mind on its own is inert. It rests in Consciousness and without Consciousness to illuminate it the mind could not think, any more than images could appear on a cinema screen without the physical light of the projector. So the first part of this meditation states a great truth: 'I AM THE INNER LIGHT WHICH PROMPTS THE MIND'. My real identity, my real 'I' is not bound up with this body and mind. It is beyond that and we have to dig deeper and deeper in meditation to reveal it.

The second part of this meditation applies to the cosmic aspect: 'I AM THE SUN WHICH LIGHTS THE UNIVERSE'. Our world cannot exist without the sun just as our mind cannot exist without Consciousness. But our sun and the billions of suns in other solar systems exist and cease to exist in Consciousness. Identified with the body, mind and senses, we feel separate, but our 'I' is not separate from the universe. The divine core of Consciousness interpenetrates the entire universe like a thread and the Consciousness which is the core of our being is the same Consciousness in which the universe abides. The yogis call this Atman — the Self — when it applies to the individual, and Brahman when it applies to the universal, but it is one and the same Consciousness.

S.M.

Recognizing the Thread
Final talk of the Annual One-Day Course

THIS TALK IS intended to do two things. First, to try to draw together some of the strands of what you have heard already today. And second, to point you towards the thread that will guide you out of the labyrinth of everyday existence — and towards a more fulfilled and fulfilling life.

As earlier speakers have suggested, there is another sort of thread that we need to recognize — one that binds us to one another; and that also supports the whole world like beads on a necklace.

The Thread of the Labyrinth

The story of Theseus and the labyrinth is a familiar one. It may become more familiar if the speaker mentions the minotaur, the half-man half-bull creature that the hero had to confront and kill. To overcome this monster, Theseus needed physical strength and courage. But none of that would have been any use if he had ended up lost in the fiendish maze. To save him from that fate, he had a thread which he unwound as he wandered the labyrinth. So when the fighting was over, it was a simple matter to follow the thread and retrace his steps.

Two things about the thread: First, Theseus's thread was supplied by someone (Ariadne) with insight, someone who realized that his inner resources of strength and courage were necessary — but not sufficient — for the task in hand. Second, a thread is a seemingly insignificant thing — it could easily be overlooked — but it has a significance well beyond its outward appearance. In that sense it is like a tiny key, that can open a huge door more easily than any amount of bashing and hammering.

Why do we need a thread? Because we are not satisfied. The yogis would say that there is nothing in the world that *can* fully satisfy us. Yoga is a voluntary process. And it is based on experience. The teachers of Yoga invite us to try, by all means, to find something in the everyday world that is fully satisfying. At the risk of sounding disrespectful, they are on a pretty safe bet. The national lottery may be an instrument of the law of karma — and one that makes selected people far wealthier than they were. But the yogis do not equate wealth with happiness. Our present condition is equivalent to an illness — for which we need a cure; or to a bad dream — from which we need to wake up.

The labyrinth is not a bad analogy. In the words of the *Bhagavad Gita:*

> Here... [in Yoga] there is one thought of a resolute nature. Many branched and endless are the thoughts of the irresolute. (Ch 2 v 41)

We can surely recognize this diagnosis. Anyone who has tried to navigate a maze will know what it feels like to have a good, logical, idea about the right way to go — and yet to end up in a succession of dead ends.

The thread is a small thing. It can easily be overlooked. But it is the route back to normality. One can make too much of myth, but it is worth remembering that the minotaur — half-man, half-bull — is symbolic of the unholy mix of rational and animal in human nature, with animal predominant. Adhyatma Yoga is a means to channel our strength in the age-old struggle against our lower nature. Like Theseus, we do not have to struggle alone. The great yogis of the past have given us a thread to follow — so that their insights can complement and guide the deployment of our inner resources.

The promise of Yoga is that we can realize that we are bound by a golden thread to God, to the Absolute. Here and now we may not be conscious of a deep affinity to the divine. But we surely feel the need for the peace and bliss that Yoga promises us.

The first speaker this morning mentioned that Yoga promises an insight into our deeper nature as well as a means to realize it. Yoga involves **meditation**, **study** and **mental** and **ethical** discipline. These are the four strands of the thread that is the yogic life. These are ancient and traditional methods, derived from the spiritual classics of the East such as the Upanishads and the *Bhagavad Gita.* Undertaken in the traditional spirit, they complement one another and the pupil's endeavours in any one of these areas support what he or she does in the others.

Meditation is the cornerstone of Yoga practice. We hope very much that you will take away with you the meditation practices given at today's course and give them a trial. We promise you that they will produce a result. They *will* make a difference.

Study of the ancient — and indeed the modern — classics of Yoga helps in at least two ways. It helps us to become familiar with the philosophy and with the tradition that supports it; and works such as *The Ramayana, The Gospel of St John, The Heart of the Eastern Mystical Teaching* — which is our teacher's biography of his own teacher, the saint Shri Dada — these books put flesh on the bones of the teachings by telling us of the lives of the great avatars and teachers. These are the great ones who lived the philosophy and whose example gives us an indication of the ideal life of Yoga.

The value of **mental discipline** to the aspiring yogi may not be so immediately obvious. But Marjorie Waterhouse, Dr Shastri's successor as Warden of Shanti Sadan, taught us that yogis need a strong will if they are to practise Yoga successfully. Her book *Training the Mind through Yoga* contains a number of helpful exercises for mind control. One very simple one is to make a conscious effort to think about a single topic for a short period of time without a break in concentration. For instance, we might try and spend three minutes thinking about trees. The actual topic chosen is not too important, but it obviously needs to be something that we won't get too excited about.

It may not sound like much of a challenge — three minutes thinking about a single topic. A mere 180 seconds. *Do* try it — and find out just how 'easy' it is! You may be surprised. And when you can manage three minutes, try *five*. And then *ten*. The ability to concentrate is invaluable in the practice of meditation. And the process of learning how to concentrate will, the speaker guarantees it, teach you something valuable about the nature of your mind.

Ethical living is the fourth essential of Yoga. We sometimes use the word *dharma* meaning 'duty' or 'right conduct'. In general, ethical questions are not cut and dried, so the speaker has chosen a relatively simple example: Stealing is one thing that we can all agree is wrong. But why? One suggestion: Christ said 'love thy neighbour as thy self'. We do not rob ourselves or knowingly do harm to ourselves. That sense of not being separate from others is the basis of yogic ethics. In essence there is no-one to rob; and no gain to be had by taking advantage of another.

In his book *Meditation: Its Theory and Practice*, our Teacher Dr Shastri gives us a key to morality and ethics. He says that the aspiring yogi should avoid those thoughts and actions that are demeaning and debasing in one's own eyes. This is not to ignore altogether the opinions of others or the dictates of society. But it is in itself a sort of discipline — listening to and seeking to develop the inner voice of conscience. Everyone has this inner voice, but we need to develop the habit of listening to it. We have all faced dilemmas in our lives, situations where we just did not know what to do for the best. That kind of indecision can be very painful. If we practise Yoga, we should, over time, develop a heightened moral sense — and find it easier to cope with such situations.

The Thread of Unity

The second speaker told us (see p55) about the gold hunter who sorts rocks into two piles, potential and useless, and put forward the view that in the case of humans it is not like that — there is gold in everyone. A golden thread unites us all. There are a few points we could usefully draw out from this analogy:

First, that the Yoga teachings are universal. They are for everyone and anyone who cares to take an interest. And we all have the qualifications to take up Yoga and succeed in it. One of the great yogis put it something like this. All are qualified to take up Yoga because we all suffer in the world; and Yoga is one sure means to become free of suffering.

Second, that for all our outward differences, we all have, at a deeper level, something very important in common. The yogis would say that that something is inner light; a spark, if you will, of the divine nature. This is one aspect of the golden thread.

Another interpretation is that God, the Absolute, is the one reality underlying all the multifarious phenomena of the empirical world and also the ground and support of all. In the *Bhagavad Gita*, the Lord Krishna says that He pervades the whole world. In a memorable phrase, He says that all is based on Him, as the beads of a necklace are supported on a thread.

Third, the difference between wisdom and information. Imagine Theseus lost in the labyrinth. How can he escape? If he has the correct *information*, he will know to take a left turning, then a right, than another right, then left... It is easy to get confused. How much better to have the *wisdom*, simply to follow the thread.

Fourth, the imperative to look deeper. And the need to calm our mind. As was said earlier, the thread is easy to overlook. The calmness we develop from following the Yoga practice will help us to find it.

Yoga is experimental, in the sense that it promises results if we follow the instructions. If Yoga were merely a theoretical system it would have no value. The 'instructions', to reiterate, are to take up meditation, to do some study and to attempt mental and ethical discipline. We recommend that you allow six weeks for your first experiment in Yoga. During that time, *something* will change. Something will improve.

To return to the illustration of our unenlightened everyday existence as a labyrinth or maze; a maze is only a puzzle to us because of our limited viewpoint. When we see it from above — e.g. from the top of a step-ladder — the way out is obvious. The teachers of Yoga have that higher standpoint, and one day we may have it also.

As the last speaker said, the age of enlightenment is something we look forward to, in the future. Science has slowly come to realize the importance of consciousness — and may yet come to appreciate that, as Yoga teaches, it is all-pervading.

Today's world is no rose garden. We only need to open a newspaper to realize that. There are many evils abroad which may seem to be permanent and unshakeable. But if you take up Yoga, you *will* be shaking them. You will be making a difference in your own being; a difference in your family and wider circle; a difference in society.

Our efforts may seem insignificant. But in truth they are anything but insignificant. It is our task to create the prior conditions for the dawn of a new age that will surprise us all. At one time we might have put all our faith in empirical science, but we are becoming increasingly aware of its limitations. The *Bhagavad Gita* calls Yoga 'The Sovereign Science'. It is one that will completely repay our faith in it.

To conclude: Yoga practice is a golden thread, a gift to us from an inspired and compassionate source. If we follow this thread, we will find release from the maze of suffering. There is also an inner thread, which is not yet visible to us, but which will become apparent if we take up Yoga. This is the thread of peace and wisdom, the thread of consciousness. Let us learn to recognize it.

S.M.R.

END OF THE ANNUAL ONE-DAY COURSE

MEDITATION PRACTICES

Breathing

Focus the mind on the navel. Take a deep breath in relaxation and, as you breathe in, imagine that you are drawing the breath up from the navel, so that you end the breath by thinking of the space between the two eyebrows. Take 21 breaths in this way.
(5 mins)

(from the book Meditation: Its Theory and Practice)

Visualisation

Visualise a candle flame in the heart centre - the hollow at the centre of the body where the ribs meet.
(5 mins)

The Text for Meditation

OM   I AM THE INNER LIGHT WHICH PROMPTS THE MIND.
I AM THE SUN WHICH LIGHTS THE WHOLE UNIVERSE. OM

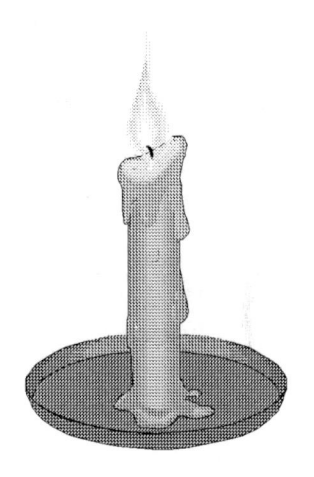

(5-10 mins)

Goodwill practice

Sit quietly and send out rays of goodwill to cover the whole world.

LIGHT A CANDLE

Light a candle in thy dark room;
It is dangerous to move about in darkness,
Which hides the beautiful vases,
The Japanese miniatures, the Mogul paintings.
Darkness conceals the Odes of Hafiz,
The sublime poetry of Valmiki.

Is it still dark?
Is not the light of one candle adequate?
Then light another candle, and yet another.
Kindle the flame of love in thy heart,
And feed it with the oil of knowledge.
There are stars, universes of peace and beauty;
There are moons more beautiful than the external one;
There is the lotus of immortality.

Kindle the flame of love in the chamber of thy heart;
Light the taper of earnest quest,
And create the light of discrimination.
No beasts, however dangerous,
Approach a fire in the forest;
No scorpions of unrequited love,
Will dare come near thee,
When there is light in thy mind.
Oh! Light a candle of love in thy heart.

H.P. Shastri